For my beloved husband Richard
who only plays with the bamboo..

For where your treasure is, there your heart will be also.

Matthew 6:21

PAINTING, PASSION
AND THE
ART OF LIFE

WRITTEN AND ILLUSTRATED BY
MICHELE BLEDSOE

outskirts
press

Painting, Passion and the Art of Life
All Rights Reserved.
Copyright © 2020 Michele Bledsoe
v2.0

The opinions expressed in this manuscript are solely the opinions of the author and do not represent the opinions or thoughts of the publisher. The author has represented and warranted full ownership and/or legal right to publish all the materials in this book.

This book may not be reproduced, transmitted, or stored in whole or in part by any means, including graphic, electronic, or mechanical without the express written consent of the publisher except in the case of brief quotations embodied in critical articles and reviews.

Outskirts Press, Inc.
http://www.outskirtspress.com

ISBN: 978-1-9772-2502-3

Cover Illustration © 2020 Michele Bledsoe. All rights reserved - used with permission.

Outskirts Press and the "OP" logo are trademarks belonging to Outskirts Press, Inc.

PRINTED IN THE UNITED STATES OF AMERICA

TABLE OF CONTENTS

ONCE UPON A TIME i

INTRODUCTION iii

BOOK ONE 1
    DEDICATION AND THE ART OF CULTIVATING THE GIFT

BOOK TWO 31
    TINY BRUSHES AND THE ART OF PASSION

BOOK THREE.. 57
    PERSONAL STORIES AND THE ART OF BEING YOURSELF

BOOK FOUR 91
    SPIRITUALITY AND THE ART OF DRAWING CLOSER TO GOD

BOOK FIVE 117
    SHARING YOUR GIFT AND THE ART OF SERVICE

ABOUT THE AUTHOR 150

ONCE UPON A TIME

I remember making a book when I was little. I vaguely recall the story had something to do with a family of animals living near a beach. I made drawings of weird dog-like creatures on pieces of paper that I folded to look like pages.

When I showed it to my grandfather,

he knelt down in front of me and told me I had a gift from God.

I was just a little girl, and believe me — My drawings were pretty simple.

Surely, if this was a gift from God..

Wouldn't my drawings be perfect?

Absolutely perfect?

Even though I was just a child, shouldn't my little book be filled with photo-realistic beach scenes and dogs so flawlessly rendered it seemed they could leap from the pages?

No.

At the time, I didn't see it..

But my grandfather was right.

INTRODUCTION

The desire to create is a gift from God.

The ceaseless passion to paint and draw has been with me since childhood..

and by embracing this gift

it has defined my path in life.

By nature,

the gift is selfless.

It has nothing to do with

the pursuit of fame and fortune..

Although these things may happen along the way,

The gift is so much more than that.

It unleashed my imagination.

It challenged my endurance and skill.

It carried me through difficult times

and comforted me when I was alone.

The gift gave me purpose and direction..

It opened a door into the deepest places of my heart

and a window to my soul.

As an artist

I've found that it's not all about me..

I am just a paintbrush in God's hand.

BOOK ONE

DEDICATION AND THE ART OF CULTIVATING THE GIFT

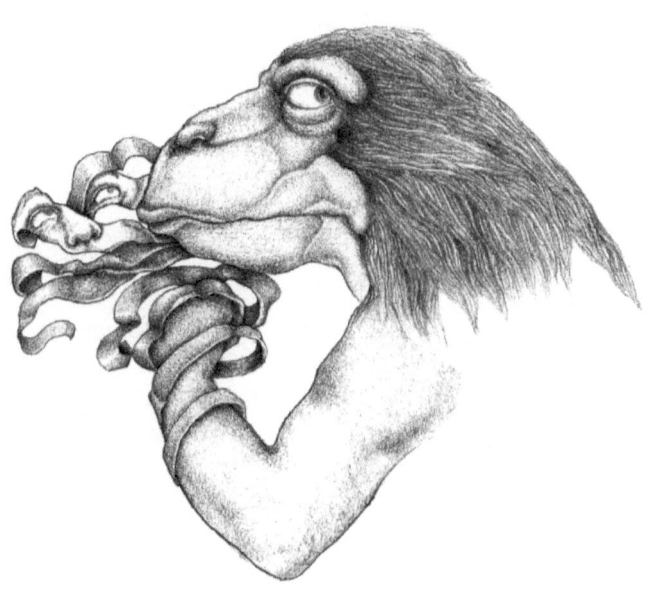

"The artist is nothing without the gift,
but the gift is nothing without the work."

Oscar Wilde

PAINTING AND THE ART OF NOT HAVING A CLUE

When I first started painting

I had no idea what I was doing..

but that didn't matter.

I just bought some basic materials

and started painting.

Finding my way through the wilderness

embracing every struggle and triumph.

It has been a glorious adventure

one painting

after another.

No experience required

to begin this magnificent journey..

all you need is

the unwavering

relentless desire

to create.

THE ART OF MAKING MISTAKES

I love to draw in pen.

Why?

Because you can't make mistakes.

Well, technically you *can* make mistakes..

but drawing in pen teaches you not to be *defeated* by mistakes.

Big difference.

Drawing in pen teaches you to be creative.

Drawing in pen teaches you to bounce back.

When mistakes do happen... and they will

do you just trash the whole thing and start over?

No.

You work through it.

You get creative.

You bounce back.

Such is life.

SIX HANDS AND THE ART OF FOLLOWING YOUR BRUSH

When I paint

I put a blob of raw umber on my palette

and start drawing on the canvas.

I don't stop to think about what I'm doing

I go wherever my paintbrush takes me.

Often it leads me into difficult territory..

Not away from it.

Hands are hard,

yet the creature that ended up on my canvas

has six of them.

So I struggle.

I fight.

I am committed to the end.

Dedicated to the direction of my gift

and the heart that guides me..

I will never give up.

Don't avoid the hard stuff.

That's how you grow.

NOT EVERYONE IS AN ARTIST

Pablo Picasso once famously said, "Every child is an artist. The problem is how to remain an artist once we grow up."

I agree with Picasso about the first part,

but the "problem" of how to remain an artist once we grow up..

is not a problem at all.

On many occasions, people have approached me at art shows telling me that they "used to draw". I always ask them, "Why did you stop?" Although the specifics may vary, the typical response is that they simply lost interest and became focused on other things. In all my years interacting with people, I have never met someone who stopped drawing against their own will. The desire just naturally faded away.

Of course it would be a struggle to "remain an artist" if you were not meant to be one.

Yes, every child draws, but not every child was meant to be an artist.

So, what's the difference?

How do you know?

Well, you just do.

Trust the gift.

CLOSING THE GAP AND THE ART OF DOING YOUR BEST

From the time when I first started drawing

I put every ounce of skill I had

into every picture I made.

Whatever the result,

Good or bad..

it was the very best I could do at the time.

Although the distance between

Where I was

and where I wanted to be

felt so far away..

giving up never crossed my mind.

That's not how it works.

The relentless drive

To keep drawing

keep pushing

To fully realize your vision..

Is unstoppable.

You will get there.

Trust the gift.

CLASSICAL GUITAR AND THE ART OF IMPOSSIBLE PURSUITS

I am a self-taught artist.

I am also a self-taught, occasional guitarist.

I like to pick out difficult pieces of music and teach myself to play them on the guitar.

Maybe that's a strange hobby for someone who can't read music and never had a lesson..

but I believe that determination and dedication can overcome any obstacle.

When I first attempted to learn "Classical Gas"

it seemed utterly impossible.

I could barely get my fingers to reach where they needed to go.

Slowly and clumsily

I fought through my frustration

one agonizing note at a time.

It was very difficult

and it sounded awful

but, I refused to give up.

It took me four years to learn "Classical Gas"

and every time I play that beautiful, complicated piece of music on my guitar

I am reminded that you can accomplish anything..

if you are willing to do what it takes to get there.

Sometimes it takes years.

Sometimes it takes a lifetime.

It's worth it.

Life is a marathon, not a sprint.

ART AND THE JOURNEY WITHIN

I really enjoy the process of painting.

I don't enjoy it because it is easy..

I enjoy the process because it is difficult.

As artists, we are explorers.

Every blank canvas is the beginning of a new journey.

Years of experience may make you stronger..

but it does not make the road any easier.

When inspiration strikes

you must go wherever it takes you.

Trust the gift.

INTERRUPTED PAINTINGS AND THE ART OF CHANGE

I was in the middle of a large painting

when life took a twist and I had to move across the country.

So I packed up my work

and carefully wrapped my easel

in blankets and brown paper.

It was a difficult transition.

By the time I was able to work on the painting again

It was practically alien to me.

I had forgotten everything.

Still early in my years as a painter

I had not yet developed a distinct palette.

I could not recognize or remember

which colors I had used

or in what combination.

This half-finished painting,

like an interrupted life...

How could I pick up where I left off?

I couldn't.

Refusing to be defeated by this overwhelming obstacle

I put my head down and got to work.

Experimenting with color

I took a leap of faith

and fought my way through.

Turns out

The painting had to change

and so did I.

SEA TURTLES AND THE ART OF BEING FEARLESS

There is no place for cowardice in art.

Like tiny sea turtles

Struggling to reach the sea..

You must trust your instincts.

It won't be easy..

But you must go where you are meant to be.

While painting,

A single dot of white on the tip of a nose

Can pop it right out of the canvas..

Whereas

Overthinking..

Or a misplaced mark

Can set you back for hours.

Whatever it is..

Do it anyway.

Make the mark

take the risk

Don't hesitate.

Artists must be fearless.

Trust the gift.

PAINTING DISASTERS AND ARTISTIC FIGHT OR FLIGHT

When I paint, I sit at my beloved easel with my palette in my lap. Once, when I was putting finishing touches on a painting – I scooted up real close to work on some detail, and something terrible happened.

My knee bumped into my easel and the painting fell face down into my palette of wet paint.

This was nothing short of a catastrophe.

But in that moment of artistic fight or flight – my instinct was to fight.

Frantically, I wiped the blobs of paint away – working quickly with my fingers and the sleeve of my shirt. I allowed myself only a few seconds to stare in horror at the massive smears of color that obliterated what was once my nearly finished painting... and immediately went back to work.

Was I going to abandon something I loved just because things got difficult?

No.

Such is life.

PAINTING DEADLINES AND THE ART OF LIFE

For the past week or so

I have been deep in the heart

of an epic painting frenzy.

Typically, I am a slow painter..

lingering over my work..

savoring every brushstroke.

But under the pressure of a deadline

I have thrown myself into the maelstrom

that comes from speeding up

the creative process.

It is a challenge of stamina

and skill.

A test of faith and trust.

Sitting at my easel for 12+ hours a day,

I have experienced almost every emotion imaginable.

It is a glorious experience..

A metaphor for life.

PRUSSIAN BLUE AND THE ART OF BEING IMPULSIVE

I have a very distinct palette...

a range of colors that I use

every time I paint.

Raw Umber

Chromium Oxide Green

Cobalt Blue

Turner's Yellow

Red Oxide

Raw Sienna..

to name a few.

I know these colors intimately;

How they react to each other..

all their moods

and subtleties..

I know them like I know

the landscape of my own heart.

But, when I started work on my painting, *Frozen Zoo*

I did something outrageously impulsive

and decided to use a new color.

Not just a little taste of it..

not just dipping my toe in the water..

Instead, I stared at that strange tube of paint in front of me

and decided to cover a *huge* portion of my canvas with it.

That was my introduction to Prussian Blue.

A tremendous leap of artistic faith..

it was an epic struggle

to incorporate this alien color into my familiar palette.

It did weird things

when I mixed it with Raw Umber.

Is that a hint of green I see?

Yellow?

I never realized that blue could be so warm.

Flailing about and lost in unfamiliar territory

I refused to back down.

By the time the painting was completed

Prussian Blue was like an old friend..

battle tested and true,

it is a welcome addition

to my comfortable palette.

There is no place for cowardice in art.

PAINTING AND THE ART OF ACCEPTING CHALLENGES

Follow your creative vision

Wherever it takes you.

No matter how difficult or impossible it seems..

Do not hesitate.

Accept the challenge

and rise up to meet it.

You were given these trials for a reason.

It is a call to arms..

An invitation to grow.

Keep fighting

and trust the gift.

You will win.

PAINTING PORTRAITS AND THE ART OF NOT LISTENING

Many artists have told me that portraits are hard.

They tell me it's difficult to get a likeness..

I don't listen.

That is why I can paint portraits

and capture a likeness.

I never stop to think whether I can or can't..

I just do.

Trust the gift.

SHARED SKETCHBOOKS AND THE ART OF ILLUSTRATING ILLNESS

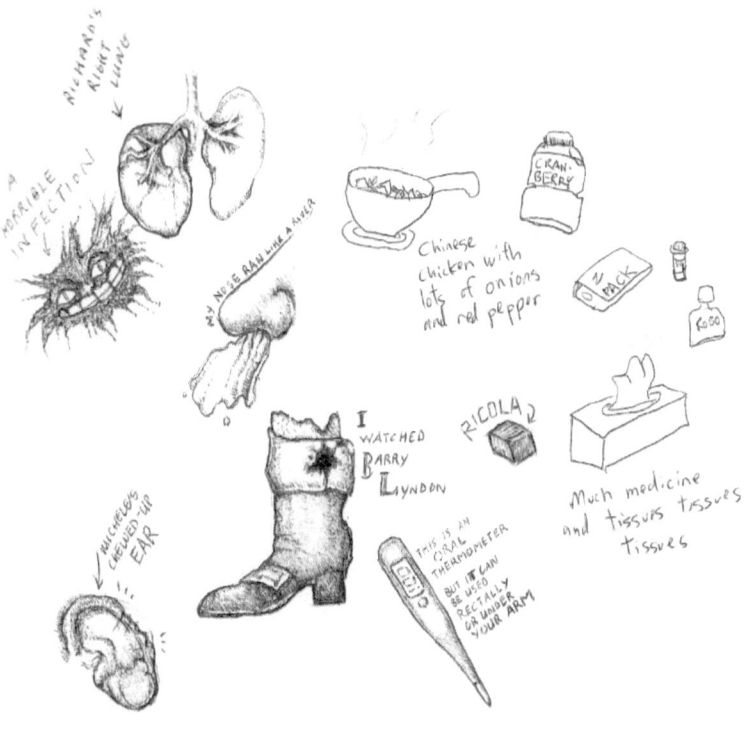

Richard and I got really sick.

We couldn't get out of bed or breathe through our noses

But that didn't stop us from drawing.

CONSTANT COMPANIONSHIP AND THE ART OF BEING ALONE

A man complimented my draftsmanship

at an art show a few years back.

Marveling over the confident lines and intriguing imagery of my paintings..

he commented that I must have had a lot of friends growing up

drawing as well as I did.

No, I told him.

In fact, it was the exact opposite.

Art thrives in isolation.

The hours upon hours

spent deep in the places where art comes from..

This is what it takes.

Art was my constant companion

My most intimate friend

And it shows on the canvas..

the magnificent results of solitude

and love

over time.

PREDESTINATION AND THE ART OF CALL WAITING

No one rolls out of bed one day

and decides to be an artist..

you were *meant* to be one.

Even if you don't answer the call for many years

it has always been there

inside you

waiting.

HITTING A WALL AND THE ART OF OVERCOMING OBSTACLES

Where to begin?

What do I make..?

Staring at a blank canvas

can be surprisingly intimidating

But there is a solution —

Pick up your brush and start painting.

Artist block happens

When you are thinking

More than doing..

So, when you hit a wall

Or encounter an obstacle

Take a leap of faith

and get to work.

INGLORIOUS ARIZONA AND THE ART OF PUSHING YOUR LIMITS

My husband Richard and I were honored to be included among the artists selected to create work for INGLORIOUS ARIZONA. In this exciting project, stories about the grittier side of Arizona's past were assigned to a selection of local artists. Once received, the artists would have about a month to create art inspired by their particular story.

One month may seem like a lot of time..

but not for me.

I am a meticulous painter..

blissfully lingering over my work with tiny brushes.

So, when I submitted samples of my work for consideration

I knew that if I were selected

I would pretty much have to paint non-stop for 30 days.

Did I hesitate?

No.

And during the magnificent painting frenzy that followed

I pushed the limits of my endurance

to the breaking point...

only to discover

that I did not break.

Trust the gift.

DRAWING AND THE SATISFACTION OF ENDLESS WORK

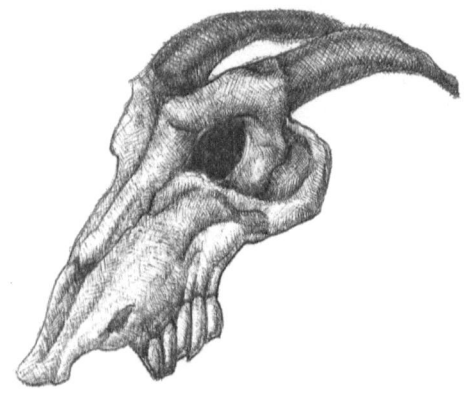

It is a pleasure to draw.

A delightful experience

that satisfies my ravenous desire to create.

The work never ends

and I am glad.

BOOK TWO

TINY BRUSHES AND THE ART OF PASSION

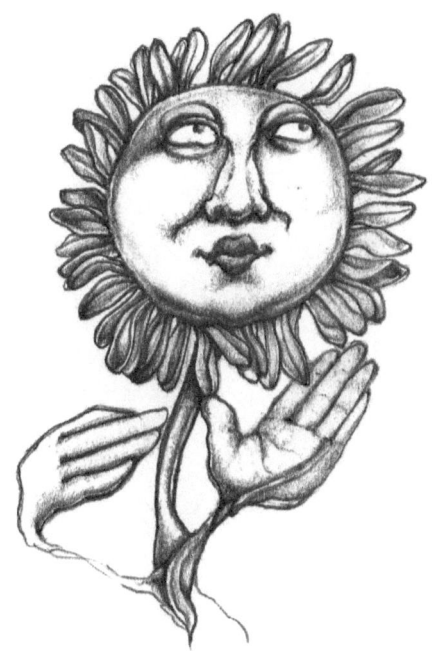

"I am seeking. I am striving. I am in it with all my heart."

Vincent van Gogh

IN ART THERE IS NO MIDDLE GROUND

I put everything I am into my art.

Doesn't matter if it is the painting of a single leaf,

or an elaborate composition I spent a thousand hours of my life on..

I pour my soul onto that canvas.

Whenever I sit in front of my easel, it is all or nothing.

There is no other way.

LITTLE BRUSHES AND THE MAGNIFICENT INEFFICIENCY OF PAINTING SLOW

I use small paintbrushes.

Makes no difference how large the canvas is,

I always use the same little brushes.

Maybe that's not very practical or efficient..

but the experience of art has nothing to do with such things.

Those who are aware of my methods often state the obvious:

"If you use bigger brushes, it won't take you so long to finish a painting."

It does take a long time.

I am a slow painter

but I wouldn't have it any other way.

I love the act of painting..

the *experience* of it.

So, I linger over my work.

I savor it.

Every little brushstroke

slowly adding layer after layer

of analogous color...

I want it to last.

A GLORIOUS PAINTING FRENZY

I have been consumed by a glorious painting frenzy.

Hours pass like minutes.

I paint and paint and paint.

Repeatedly sipping from an empty cup

forgetting that I finished drinking my coffee 2 hours ago.

No time to take a shower.

I forget to eat..

or move.

When I lean back in my chair

my back cracks all the way down my spine like dominoes falling

and then I start painting again.

INSPIRATION AND THE ART OF MISSING A DEADLINE

I have a deadline coming up..

an art exhibit in November.

That means, I have less than a month to finish the painting I am working on for the show..

Or not.

When I started this painting

it immediately exploded into something deeply complex

and intensely personal.

The last thing on my mind was the approaching deadline.

I suppose it would have been more practical to consider the time constraints

maybe make something smaller or less elaborate..

But art does not fit neatly into such parameters.

Art cannot be contained.

It will become what it needs to be.

When inspiration seizes you like some fiery angel

don't interfere..

just let it take you.

ART DEPRIVATION AND THE NECESSITY OF PAINTING

I love to paint.

I *need* to paint..

but sometimes life intervenes

and pulls me from my easel.

I feel unbalanced.

Irritable.

Something is off.

I am suffering from art deprivation..

Like some kind of

horrible sleep deficiency..

there is an almost physical

longing to dream.

As artists, it is necessary to make time

to create..

our lives depend on it.

PAINTING AND THE ART OF BURNING FROM WITHIN

Hard to tell

from watching me paint

that I am in the grip

of a glorious painting frenzy.

Outside

I am sitting quietly at my easel

slowly

meticulously

adding layer after layer

of analogous color..

Inside

my soul is on fire.

PERSERVERANCE AND THE IRRESISTABLE FORCE OF ART

I hurt my hand.

Swollen, painful...

Nothing spectacular.

Immobilization is needed — to give it time to heal

But I take the brace off to paint.

I can't help myself.

I just started a new painting..

and I am consumed with the joy of it.

The hand?

Yes, it hurts when I paint..

but it would hurt more if I stopped.

PAINTING AND THE ART OF RELATIVITY

Every time I sit in front of a blank canvas

I pour everything I've got into it.

Everything.

Doesn't matter if it's only 3" x 5"..

I will release my universe

into something

that can fit into the palm

of my hand.

There is no other way..

It's all or nothing.

Just as all the mystery and fullness of life

can squeeze itself into a single

moment..

Such is the power of art.

PAINTING AND THE ART OF DECOMPRESSION SICKNESS

Lost myself again.

Just sank a little too deep

below the surface for a while..

and stayed there too long.

Art will do that to you.

Perhaps I have the painter-bends..

some kind of decompression sickness

that artists get

when they come up for air.

All I want to do is go back.

THE HUMAN CONDITION AND THE ART OF CAPTURING TIME

The act of painting is a remarkable experience.

It is the human condition

rendered in brushstrokes..

Captured on canvas;

Frozen in time.

ULTRAMARINE BLUE AND THE UNBEARABLE BEAUTY OF GRAY

Welcome Ultramarine Blue

to the collection of colors that make up my palette.

I am just beginning to explore your mysteries.

You make the most exquisite gray

when mixed with my beloved

Raw Umber..

but after adding the tiniest dot of Titanium White..

I hold back.

I see where this is going..

it is the promise of almost unbearable beauty.

One last, long breath

And then

Bliss.

STOCKPILING PENS AND THE ART OF TREATING YOURSELF

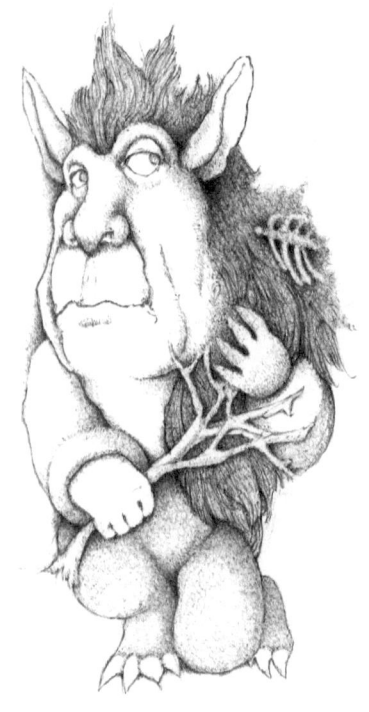

I bought myself a present the other day..

Another 2-pack of my favorite pens from the local drugstore.

I can never have enough.

LIFE, WORK AND THE ART OF A HOME STUDIO

No matter where I live

There is always a place to paint.

A dedicated space to create is a vital part of my living environment.

My studio has been in a kitchen

a basement

a corner of my bedroom..

It is always near me.

Once, I had a studio space above the gallery that represented my work..

I didn't like it.

Having to get dressed, get in my car and drive to another location

Every time I wanted to paint?

Ridiculous.

I have left my home to drive to the various day jobs I've had..

But art is not work.

It is life.

FINISHED PAINTINGS AND THE ART OF LETTING GO

I am nearing the end of my painting.

"It looks done." Richard says

There is so much left to do, I reply

I can't help myself.

This painting and I have been through a lot together

and after 2 years of working on it..

I'm not ready to stop.

So I sit at my easel

With my face pushed up against the canvas

Exploring every inch of its surface..

Examining every line

Every delicate transition.

I pick up my tiny brush

And retrace my path..

One last time

before letting go.

DOLLHOUSE PAINTINGS AND THE ART OF GIVING YOUR ALL

My sister asked me to make a painting

to hang in her dollhouse.

So I did.

With squinting eyes,

I leaned in close

and poured my soul onto that tiny canvas.

Is it a waste of time to put so much of myself

into a 2" x 2" square?

No.

Art is all or nothing.

Every time.

NEGATIVE SPACE AND THE ART OF BEING YOURSELF

Just as the negative space

around an object

will define its shape..

You can tell a lot about a person

by what they like.

These things reveal something about us..

But art is different.

More than just a human-shaped outline

formed by the things we respond to..

When you create art

it *is* you.

CHEMICAL REACTIONS AND THE ART OF CONNECTION

When you connect with a piece of art

you know it.

It is a startling revelation..

visceral

and immediate.

Like a chemical reaction

between two powerful elements..

when it happens

you are changed forever.

STARGAZING AND THE ART OF TINY DRAWINGS

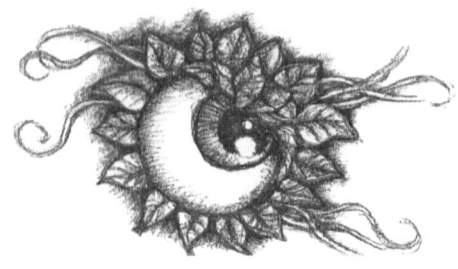

My sketchbooks are filled

with tiny drawings..

Shining like weird little stars

throughout the journey of my life.

PAINTING AND THE GLORIOUS BEAT OF THE UNCHANGEABLE HEART

The desire to create is a gift from God.

Regardless of where my path takes me

this will not change.

When my heart stops beating

I will stop painting.

Simple as that.

BOOK THREE

PERSONAL STORIES AND THE ART OF BEING YOURSELF

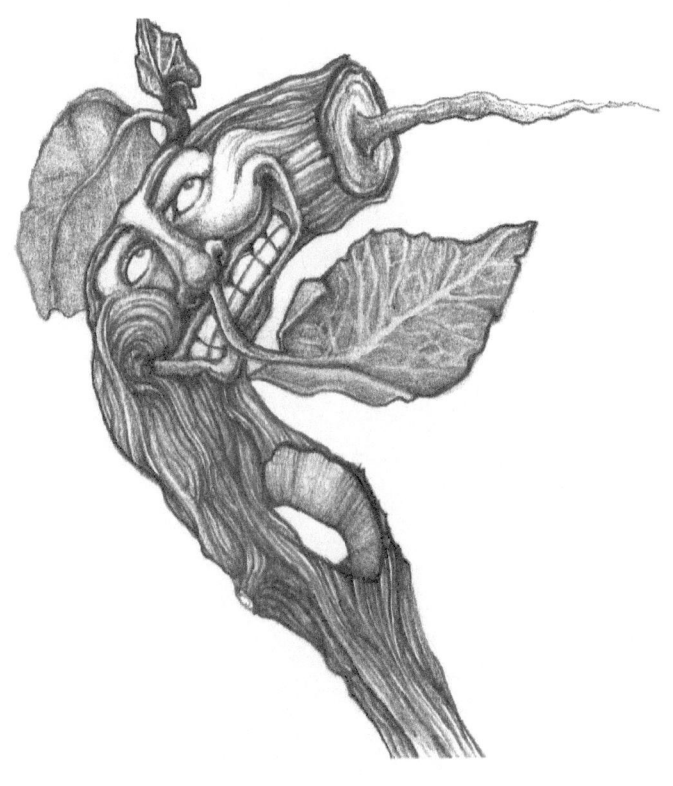

"I am interested in art as a means of living a life; not as a means of making a living."

Robert Henri

MY EASEL AND I: A LOVE STORY

For the first 24 years of my life, I drew pictures. Pencils, pens and paper were my only art supplies. The huge callus on the middle finger of my right hand was a testament to the decades I spent feverishly pouring my imagination out onto pieces of paper. As a self-taught artist, it never occurred to me to use anything other than the tools that were readily available. Why would I want anything else? I was happy.

The Christmas before he died, my father bought me an easel.

In other words, he saved my life.

Since I had never painted before, on Christmas morning I stood before that strange metal object in front of me with my mouth hanging open. My father went on to explain how much he wanted to give me an easel — describing his amusing trip to the local art supply store to buy something he knew nothing about. At the time, he didn't even know what it was called. My father told me that all the easels were made of wood, except the one he bought. He gave me a solid steel easel because he wanted it "to last forever."

Words cannot express the depth of my love for my father. When he died, it tore me apart. That easel became the rock that I clung to through the maelstrom of my grief, and I taught myself how to paint.

I painted as if my life depended on it… and it did.

That was over 25 years ago, and I have been painting ever since. Now, I understand that there are easels out there that would probably better suit my method and my materials — but for me, there will never be another easel other than the one my father gave me. Every single one of my paintings was made on that easel, and I wouldn't have it any other way.

It is going to last forever.

BRUSH HAIRS, IMPERFECTION AND THE ART OF BEING HUMAN

Inside an art museum, when you look at the people around you, you can always tell who the artists are.

They are the ones trying to push their faces up against the artwork. Balancing gracefully over velvet ropes to lean in as close as possible to the art. They examine every inch of a painting.. every brushstroke. The tiniest detail cannot escape their inquisitive, hungry eyes..

At least until security tells them they need to take a few steps back.

Maybe it's just me.

At the National Gallery of Art in Washington D.C., as I was leaning in to examine *The Human Condition* (*La Condition Humaine*) by surrealist painter, René Magritte... I noticed something astounding.

Near a corner of this amazing work of art, there was a brush hair stuck in the paint.

A brush hair stuck in the paint!

Sometimes, that happens to me, too.

Suddenly, I realized that even René Magritte was not above experiencing the same little moments of imperfection during the artistic process that I experience. He was not some unearthly creature performing feats of flawless skill and mastery over his materials...

He was simply another artist

passionate and imperfect

just like me.

Art has nothing to do with perfection..

Art is all about being human.

MR. CRAZY AND THE APPEARANCE OF BLACKBERRIES

My dog Gunther was my constant companion for 11 1/2 years. I first held him in my hands when he was a week old. Dalmatians do not have spots when they're born — so he looked like a chubby white rat. Gunther was my beloved child.

Like most dogs, Gunther had many nicknames. Lumpy, Dog-head, Goonar ... and my favorite, Mr. Crazy. That is what I called him when he was exceptionally happy — which was very often. Mr. Crazy would burst into a room, flinging toys.. tongue flapping and tail wagging like a propeller. Watching him prance and leap around the house filled me with joy.

That was many years ago.

Hanging in my studio next to my easel

Is a painting I call *Mr. Crazy's Lament*..

It is what I was working on while making the decision to put Gunther down.

During that painful, difficult time

I painted and painted.

I poured my heart out onto that canvas.

That was the first time a blackberry appeared in my paintings.

I remember sitting on a stool in my kitchen.. lost in thought. My sister came in — she had brought me blackberries. So I sat there at the table — eating blackberries and petting my beloved Gunther.

I held one of the berries in the palm of my hand. It was so delicate and fragile. This dark and beautiful object tasted so sweet.

I put it in my mouth — just for a moment..

and then it was gone.

ART AND THE PROXIMITY OF CURIOUS OBJECTS

My husband is always telling me to take a picture of the weird collection of items I have on the tray of my easel.

I'm not exactly sure what the actual purpose is for that little shelf-like area..

but it is where I keep all my favorite stuff.

Polished rocks, glass marbles and rusty keys.

Floppy-limbed Micronauts, the metal license tabs from Gunther's collar and my father's college ring.

My art studio is filled with strange little objects that have captured my attention..

but you can tell how much I like something by how close it gets to my easel.

CAT PORTRAITS AND THE ART OF BEING SELFLESS

Recently, I put aside my work in progress..

and ignored a looming deadline

to pour myself into a special request —

A portrait of my sister's beloved cat, Munchkin

who had just passed away.

This is what art is all about.

Not the galleries and the exhibits.

Not the personal attention

and public exposure...

it's about the gift

and what you choose to do with it.

RUSSIAN SNAILS AND THE UNIVERSAL LANGUAGE OF ART

My art has never been so far from home before..

It's a small painting of a snail,

but this little creature

has managed to travel a great distance.

My husband and I are honored to have our work on display in Moscow, Russia..

We do not speak Russian,

but our paintings do.

LOST BOOKS AND THE MEASURE OF SUCCESS

The ONCE-UPON-A-TIME Storybook was the best-loved book of my childhood.

Never heard of it?

Well, you're not alone.

Unlike the works of Dr. Seuss, Maurice Sendak and Shel Silverstein, this storybook has slipped away into oblivion. Just another lost book that could not withstand the test of time..

but not really.

I loved this book so deeply and completely as a child, but as I grew older.. I started to forget.

I forgot the title. I forgot the stories. I forgot the name of the author..

but I never forgot the illustrations.

Those pictures haunted me.

So, I began a search that would last for 20 years.

I prowled endlessly through the children's section of every used book store I could find. I had no information on what I was looking for other than the memory of the wondrous images that were burned into my heart. When eBay came along, I spent thousands of hours searching in the middle of the night.. desperately plugging in keywords in an attempt to describe the pictures I cherished. A pine tree with golden leaves. A dragon and a monkey.

It seemed impossible… but I refused to give up.

To make a long story short, I found the book.

The ONCE-UPON-A-TIME Storybook was originally published in 1958, and the author and the illustrator of this beloved book are probably long gone.

Maybe they never achieved fame and fortune. Maybe they never realized that their book could create such a lasting impression.

And maybe they never knew

that they helped inspire a child to become an artist.

Success is not measured in dollar signs.

UNEXPECTED EXHIBITS AND THE ART OF A FATHER'S LOVE

In college, I decided to enter some of my drawings in a big student art show. I was not taking any art classes, but I wanted to see if my work could hold its own with a bunch of people majoring in art. I asked if the competition was open to all students, or just *art* students. An odd request, but they said it was open to all college students. That included me.

I entered five drawings — work I had done... doing what I do all the time. Sitting in my bedroom drawing and drawing. Like I had done since forever.

This was at a time when I kept my art mostly to myself. I did not run to show my drawings to my family every time I made something. Most of my work was done in secret — drawing into the night, under a bending lamp.

When I found out that all five pieces had been accepted — I was shocked. It was unexpected. Almost guiltily, I told my father that I was going to be in an art show.

The room was filled with drawings — floor to ceiling. It was packed with art students and their friends. Everyone was talking to each other, but I stuck close to my family. My father knew how much I loved to draw... he had watched me grow up. I loved my father dearly – and although he had not seen any of my recent drawings — I wanted to see if he could recognize them.

I *needed* him to, but was afraid that he wouldn't.

So, in that huge room with hundreds of drawings, I asked my father if he could pick out the ones I made. I used a joking, challenging tone — attempting to hide the enormity of how much it meant to me. My father saw right through me. He gave me a look — a small, knowing smile.. narrowing his eyes. He turned slowly – scanning the walls and quickly located each one of my drawings. "That one," he said, pointing. "And that one, that one, that one… and that one." I was astounded. How could he do that so quickly, so effortlessly as if picking my face out of a crowd?

Easy.

My father knew me..

Therefore, he knew my art.

To him, they were one and the same.

SHARED SKETCHBOOKS AND THE ART OF EATING MICE

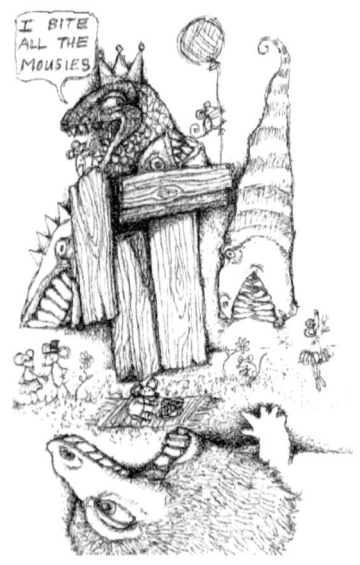

I love when people draw with me.

Passing my sketchbook back and forth..

It is a conversation without words.

I was very pleased by the adorable mice

My sister drew...

so much so that every time she added one

I created something to eat it.

I think I missed the ballerina on the right.

WHEN YOU CAN'T MAKE UP YOUR MIND... PAINT WITH YOUR HEART

When I was invited to participate in the upcoming exhibit, BOOKED: Contemporary Literary Art, I got a really late start on my painting. The exhibit is a group show which embraces the art of the story teller, and pays tribute to beloved authors whose works have moved us, inspired us, and enriched our lives.

The problem was — I couldn't make up my mind.

I love to read, and have so many favorite books. The deadline was approaching, but I just couldn't decide which one to choose.

It occurred to me that I was thinking too much.

So I stopped using my head and painted with my heart.

We Need to Talk About Kevin by Lionel Shriver is a brutal book. Horrific, yet beautifully written. It took me by surprise.. and left me wandering around stunned for days after I finished it.

This is where my art wanted to take me..

and when I let go

it stopped being the painting I thought I should do

and became the painting I was meant to do.

Big difference.

PAINTING UNDER A DEADLINE AND THE ART OF BEING OBLIVIOUS

Recently, my husband and I took part

in a group art session where we had about an hour

to create a painting.

When time was up,

Richard created a beautiful painting of an octopus

and I had painted a single, small leaf in the corner of my otherwise blank canvas.

Usually, I do not participate in this kind of event..

I am a slow painter.

Oblivious to the passing of time,

and unconcerned by the expectation to finish my work..

I picked up my paintbrush

put my head down

and disappeared.

UNFINISHED SKETCHES AND THE ART OF FRIENDSHIP

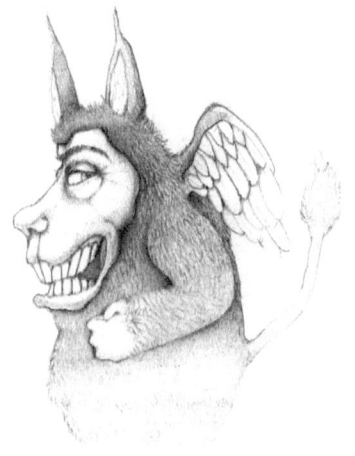

My sketchbooks are filled with tiny works in progress..

I flip through the pages

And return to them again and again

Like old friends.

IT ONLY LOOKS EMPTY ON THE OUTSIDE

Years ago, I had a studio space above the art gallery that was representing my work. It was a large, open space occupied by several other artists. I was fascinated by all the little environments these artists created for themselves — tables littered with weird objects, drapery, stacks of art books and reference materials. The walls surrounding each area were plastered with photographs, photocopies and rough sketches of works in progress.

When I was alone, I would secretly wander around from space to space, examining everyone's work and the little worlds they had created for themselves.

One evening, one of the other artists approached me. Apparently, he too enjoyed looking at everyone's stuff. He was curious why my work area was completely empty. Nothing but an easel and a chair facing a blank white wall.

Everything I need exists within the vast universe of my imagination. My work area is a place without limits or boundaries.

It only looks empty on the outside.

SMALL THINGS WITH GREAT LOVE

I have made some large paintings in my time, but mostly I prefer to work small.

I like to scoot up real close to my canvas and work lovingly with my tiny brushes for hours on end.. applying layer after layer of color. It is an intensely intimate experience that I enjoy very much.

Throughout my years of exhibiting work in galleries, I have had many people tell me that I should paint larger. Explaining to me that larger work would have more of a presence... would get more attention somehow. In group shows, my little paintings may be overlooked... hiding away in corners.. lost in the shadow of larger pieces.

Sure, I imagine there are many people who go through life and only notice the big things.

Tall buildings. Monster trucks. Large paintings. Huge sculptures.

But there are also people out there who will notice a tiny flower reaching out through a crack in the pavement of a crowded parking lot.

I guess I am one of those people.

Little moments of beauty are everywhere.. but they are only visible to those who will take the time to look closer.

So, I will continue to make my small paintings..

with great love.

SKETCHBOOKS AND THE PEOPLE YOU FIND THERE

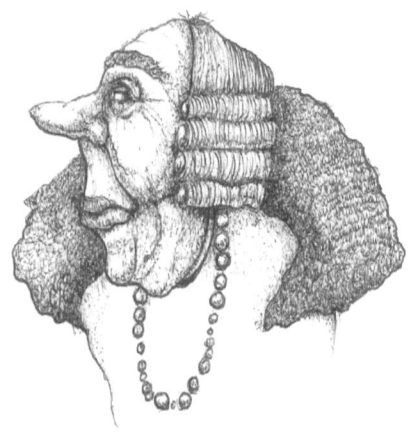

Who are these people

Who turn up in my sketchbooks?

I'm not sure..

But I am always glad to see them.

TUNNEL VISION AND UPSIDE DOWN PAINTINGS

I often develop tunnel vision while I am working..

I become so focused on the details

that I can't even see my painting anymore.

My solution to this is to turn the painting upside down

look at it a different way

find a new perspective..

and then I can see it again.

Such is life.

PAPER BAGS AND THE ART OF MAKING LUNCH

When I was in my early teens, my two younger sisters were in grade school. Every morning I would spend a few minutes preparing their lunch — and every evening I would set aside a few hours to decorate their paper lunch bags.

Gathering my collection of colored markers, I sat at the kitchen table drawing animals and bumble bees, strange creatures, flowers and unicorns. I took my time. Each one unique. More meaningful than assembling a couple of peanut butter and jelly sandwiches, the endless stream of paper bag art was my way of showing them how much I loved them.

This is what art is all about.

I remember how pleased I was when one of my sisters came home and told me someone gave her a chocolate cupcake in exchange for one of my lunch bags.

Love spreads.

BUSINESS TRAVEL AND THE ART OF THE BREAKFAST BUFFET

Growing up, whenever I was stressed or lonely..

I would draw.

Decades later, not much had changed.

While working as the Quality Manager for an international company, my position involved occasional and much dreaded business travel out of state. I hated being away from home. Having to spend a week in Virginia to prepare their office for an important certification audit... I was completely out of my comfort zone. Feeling weird and out of place among the senior management, I seized every opportunity to draw.

They put us up in a nice hotel in Richmond. Every morning we would meet at the extravagant breakfast buffet before carpooling over to the facility.

I was always the first one there.

Sequestered away in a corner behind a stack of manuals and manila folders..

I kept my head down, engrossed in my work.

The executives, department heads and senior management left me alone... assuming I was busy taking notes, reviewing documents and studying procedures in order to prepare for the day ahead.

Nope.

I was drawing a grotesque tree-person covered in bark and curling leaves.

Drawing helped me feel more focused,

More confident..

more like myself.

We passed the audit.

PAINTING AND THE ART OF PARKING LOT TREASURE HUNTS

During breaks at work

I wander around the parking lot

looking for treasure.

Pinecones,

curling leaves

twisted twigs

a dead bee

a butterfly wing..

They follow me home

and sneak into my paintings.

BLUE MAMMOTHS AND THE ART OF COLLABORATION

The first time Richard and I collaborated on a painting we divided the canvas in half diagonally. He took the upper right corner, and I took the lower left.

We would work within our own boundaries and come together where the two halves meet.

It was exciting.

I went first — Painting a jointed figure rising from carved wooden pedestals

(A recurring theme I obsessively explore in my own work).

After delicately defining the figure and basic shapes

I handed it to Richard and returned to my work in progress.

Behind me — Richard worked quickly,

Filling his quadrant with strong brushstrokes and vibrant colors.

When he handed it back to me, my eyes grew wide as I examined the bright blue, shaggy head looming benevolently over the figure I had created.

"A mammoth?" I said, incredulously.

Richard smiled.

I was momentarily stunned by the appearance of this unexpected guest

into a world usually occupied only by me.

Then my heart quickened..

Discovering Richard there on the same canvas was like encountering him in the magnificent landscape of a shared dream.

Such an intimate experience to share as husband and wife..

A love song between two painters.

BOOK FOUR

SPIRITUALITY AND THE ART OF DRAWING CLOSER TO GOD

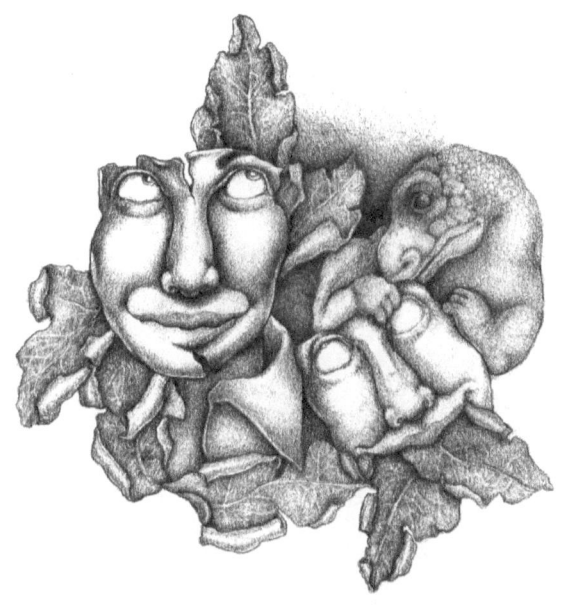

"When I work, and in my art, I hold hands with God."

Robert Mapplethorpe

PAINTING AND THE ART OF CONVERSATION

When I paint

I don't make preliminary sketches

I don't plan anything out beforehand..

I just sit at my easel

and dream.

It is a spontaneous conversation..

an intimate, spiritual exchange

between myself and God.

REPETITION AND THE ART OF PAINTED PRAYERS

Mixed in with what I create from my imagination..

my paintings are filled with objects from the natural world.

Leaves

blackberries

gnarled branches

crumbling stone

wood

seed pods

I love these things.

But, it is not enough just to look at them

or hold them in my hands…

I need to *experience* them.

I need to know them intimately.

I need to pour out my love for these things

that capture my heart.

They become part of my language of symbols.

A visual prayer.

I paint them again and again

and again..

A love song to God.

THE PAINTER, THE PAINTING AND THE ART OF LOOKING DEEPER

Once upon a time

a woman bought one of my little paintings.

When I came inside to meet her

she was surprised.

She said I did not look at all

like she expected.

Clearly, she did not look deep enough.

I look exactly like my paintings.

The body I walk around in has nothing to do with it.

VISIONARY PAINTING AND THE GLORIOUS MYSTERY OF A STRANGER'S HEART

I am often surprised

when people have a hard time identifying

what is going on in my paintings.

It happens a lot.

"What is that... a face?"

they would ask..

squinting at my work.

"Is that part of a tree...?"

I didn't understand

why not everyone could see what I was seeing..

But, then again..

I suppose it would be somewhat disorienting

to find yourself thrust

without warning

into the deepest places

of a stranger's heart.

Such is the power of art.

THE ART OF BROKEN GLASSES

While painting the other day

A lens popped out of my reading/painting glasses

And landed on my palette.

In other words

I painted so hard, my glasses broke.

As it is now

I have to tear myself away from my easel

to perform the simplest tasks —

eating

showering

refilling my empty coffee cup..

but now I had to leave the house

and get new glasses.

As I drove around

I noticed

the further away I was from my painting

the more anxious I became.

I was longing to go back to it..

Back to my studio

Back to my painting

Back at my easel

where I feel closest to God.

SELF-PORTRAITS, SPIRITUALITY AND THE ART OF BREAKING FREE

Every work of art is a self-portrait of the artist who created it.

Sometimes this is obvious..

other times, it is not.

I have included many representations of myself in my paintings..

A strange figure formed out of sculpted wood with jointed arms. Or some mysterious organic construction of tangled branches and swirling leaves.

Sometimes, I wear my human face.

Maybe these depictions are not so recognizable to the casual observer..

but I really don't consider the flesh I walk around in

as all there is to "myself".

We are so much more than that.

We are spiritual beings trapped in the body of a dying animal..

But through art, we can break free.

SELF-PORTRAITS AND THE FACE YOU FIND THERE

Regardless of who or what ends up on my canvas

everything is a self-portrait.

Everything.

Sometimes, it is not so obvious..

other times, it is.

Art goes much deeper than the surface of our skin..

and sometimes the face you find there

is not a face at all.

SEEMINGLY RANDOM OBJECTS AND THE REMARKABLE MYSTERY OF ART

I don't plan out my paintings.

No preconceived ideas. No preliminary sketches.

I just sit in front of a blank canvas and start drawing.

A strange thing happens when you work this way..

You become a conduit.

Those seemingly random objects form a mysterious language of symbols. On the surface, a painting may appear to be very simple and straightforward… but underneath, it communicates on a much deeper level. Far greater than the sum of its parts — art explores the shared experience of the human condition.

So, I am not going to dissect my paintings, examining each separate element, providing a simple explanation for every individual object it contains..

It doesn't work that way.

Art is not a puzzle to be solved..

it is a mystery to be contemplated.

Such is life.

STUDIO SPACE AND THE ART OF BEING INVISIBLE

My husband and I are both painters.

The first room you see when you enter our house is the art studio..

One half is mine

and one half is Richard's.

This beautiful little space I have created for myself

can only be seen from the outside;

because when I am painting

everything disappears..

including me.

LEAVES, RIBBONS AND THE ART OF REPEATING MYSELF

Occasionally, my sisters tease me about my paintings.

"Another leaf, Michele?"

"Ribbons... again?"

Yes.

Often my paintings

take me back

over and over again

to leaves and branches..

to seed pods and swirling ribbons.

Another blackberry.

Another mask.

Maybe to the casual observer

I am repeating myself.

But as I caress these beloved objects

that appear beneath my paintbrush,

they form a mysterious language of symbols..

An intimate, spiritual conversation

that only the heart understands.

DON'T BE AFRAID OF THE DARK

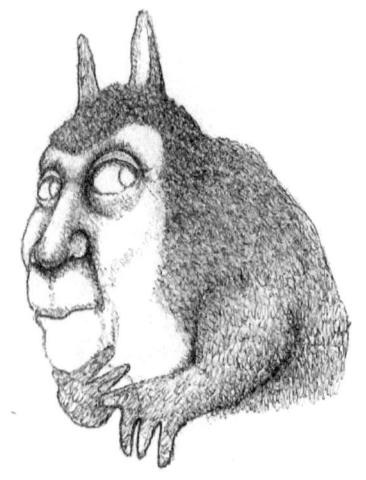

Dig deep.

Have no fear of what you find there

It's part of who you are.

Let it out

And don't be afraid of the dark.

THE ART OF PAINTING BELOW THE SURFACE

If you look at a photograph of me

you see the face I wear,

the body I walk around in

and a few items of clothing;

unlike my paintings..

which show you what I look like

on the inside.

A CONVERSATION WITH GOD

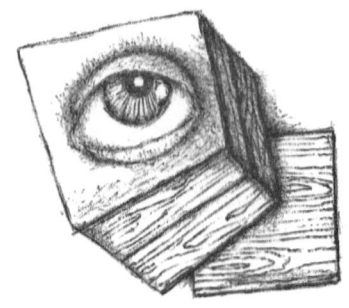

Art is the language of the spirit..

A conversation with God.

PAINTING AND THE MEASURE OF LIFE

I am not concerned with

The crow's feet around my eyes

or the gray in my hair..

I think of growing older

As it relates to my paintings.

I look back at the art of my 20s

The art of my 30s

And 40s

And 50s..

Each passing year

My creative vision has grown clearer

details are sharper

My compositions stronger

The colors more vivid

Transitions are smoother

It is the story of my artistic journey

As I draw closer

And closer

To God.

PAINTING AND THE ART OF FINDING GOD

With paintbrush in hand

I go to the place

where art flows.

Deep in these depths

I have explored my heart..

as symbols and imagery

Intertwine with memory

and spill across my canvas;

I lose myself

completely

And find God there.

STEVE GOMPF AND THE GLORIOUS BEAT OF AN UNDYING HEART

We have a lot of Steve's art in our house..

so many beautiful objects

he has given to us throughout the years.

I stare at this collection of artifacts..

touch them

and hold them in my hands.

My friend is gone..

But part of him still remains.

When you pour so much love into your art

It lingers..

Those little moments of beauty

Are left behind..

Holding within them

The heart of the artist who created it.

MIGRAINE HEADACHES AND THE ART OF PAIN

Excruciating headache

since 2:00 am

curled up

hand clamped over my eye

to keep it from popping out of my skull

beneath the unyielding pressure.

It went on and on

for hours and hours

coming in terrible waves..

When relief came

I was bursting with gratitude..

how wonderful it is

when pain stops.

So I ran to my easel

and painted and painted

with such great joy..

The headache did not return..

banished like a demon

in the light of God's gift.

NEGLECTED PAINTINGS AND THE ART OF DOING LAUNDRY

Life got busy.

Really busy.

It happens..

but I let it pull me from my easel

for too long.

That was a mistake.

Suffice it to say

I was no longer myself..

I had become

an unbalanced load of laundry

thumping and banging away...

So, I ran to my neglected painting

to set things right

and threw myself into it

with wild abandon

falling fearlessly

and gratefully

into the glorious embrace

of God's gift.

DIVINE INTERVENTION AND THE UNEXPECTED MIRACLE OF GIANT LEAPS

The slow and steady progression

that occurs

As you hone your skills

is inevitable.

The more you draw

The better you get.

Yet sometimes in the space between paintings

there is a huge leap of improvement..

a dramatic evolution

that appears in my work like a miracle.

It is Divine intervention..

Removing years from my artistic journey

to get me where I need to be.

And as I stare in wonder at my canvas

I am reminded again

That I am not alone.

BOOK FIVE

SHARING YOUR GIFT AND THE ART OF SERVICE

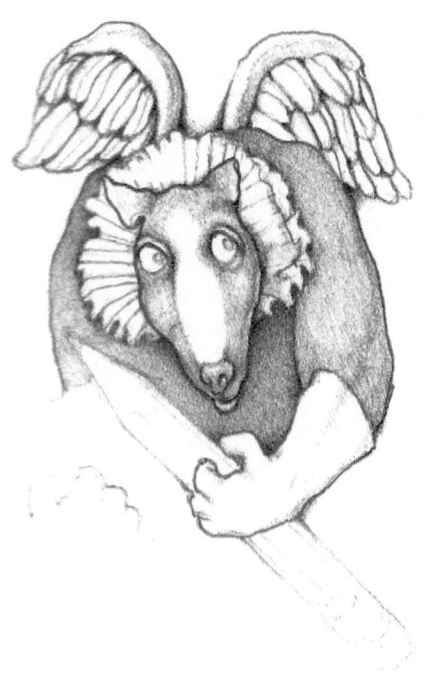

"Your talent is God's gift to you. What you
do with it is your gift back to God."

Leo Buscaglia

OPPORTUNITY, WEALTH AND THE ART OF SERVICE

There was a period of time

where my paintings were on display every month..

but I felt myself pulled in a different direction.

I still participate in exhibits occasionally

but my focus has been more on

what good can I do through *sharing* my talents

rather than how much money can I make

by selling them.

Through service I've found that

the opportunities are endless..

and the results make you rich beyond measure.

PENS, PENCILS AND IMAGINATION

I remember the first summer I volunteered to teach art to a group of inner city kids in downtown Phoenix.

Sure, I suppose it would have been good to give those underprivileged children the rare opportunity to experiment with materials they would not normally have access to... a variety of paints, pastels and charcoal. Surfaces like canvas, watercolor paper and Bristol board.

But that was not the message I wanted to share.

When I was a child, all I did was draw pictures. I used pens, pencils and whatever paper I could get my hands on. This was all I needed to make my imagination soar. So, when I walked into class that first day – that's what I brought.

If I had provided these kids with fancy supplies, maybe they would think they couldn't make art without expensive materials.

I wanted them to understand that they could continue to make art long after the class was over..

with materials they could easily obtain.

Art is for everyone.

You don't need expensive supplies to make art. All you need is a pen or pencil, a piece of paper and your imagination.

BALL POINT PENS AND THE ART OF BANISHING BOREDOM

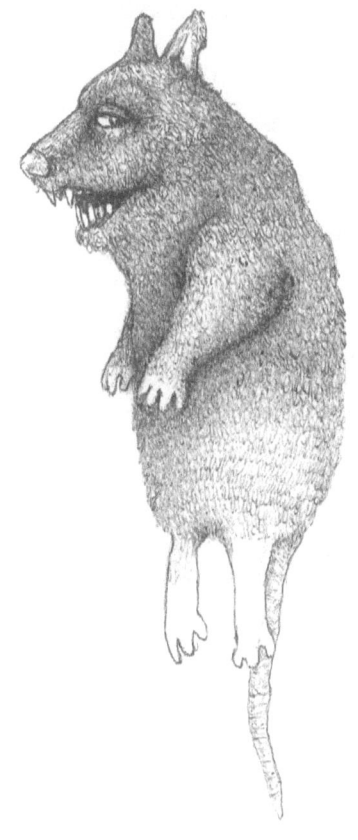

I am never bored with a pen in my hand..

SECRET GALLERIES AND THE ART OF HOME REPAIRS

We had an art show a few weeks ago

with a single attendee..

the handyman who came to repair our wall.

He examined the paintings that surrounded him

while he worked..

and as the plaster dried

he walked around

staring at all the art.

He spoke to us about our paintings

and shared stories of his own collection of art..

his father's landscape paintings

which he treasured.

As he was leaving

he thanked us for the experience

and his unexpected trip

into an art exhibit.

This is art the way it is meant to be

not cloistered away in a sterile, white-walled gallery

but as a part of everyday life..

living in our homes

like family.

THE RETURN OF BOO RADLEY

In *To Kill A Mockingbird*, Boo Radley left gifts for Jem and Scout in the knothole of an old, oak tree. He wanted the children to be aware of his presence, to understand that he cared for them, and to know that he was watching out for them.

Once upon a time I lived in a one-bedroom apartment with my dog, Gunther. In the center of the complex, there was a large grassy area surrounding a sandbox where the kids could play. Scattered on the ground, I would find some of the largest and most beautiful pinecones I had ever seen. Whenever I took Gunther for a walk, I would grab a couple and bring them back to my apartment to marvel over.

One day, I noticed a little girl playing alone in the sandbox with a large pile of pinecones. I smiled to myself. This child and I shared a love of pinecones. Later, I noticed a pile of pinecones on the open patio of one of the nearby apartments. I knew that was where the little girl lived.

That night, in a frenzy of inspiration, I took one of the pinecones from my collection and painted it a rich, deep blue with tips of vibrant green. I took my time, sitting at my easel – intent on turning the pinecone into something magical. At about 3am, I grabbed my dog and took a walk over to the girl's apartment. I left the painted pinecone on the top of her pile and went back home.

The next morning, I walked my dog past the apartment again – and the pinecone was gone.

This is where I got really creative.

To make a long story short, the pinecones got much more elaborate. I bought glitter, rhinestones, small plastic animals, ribbons and other assorted materials to incorporate into my pinecone masterpieces. Every week or so, I would leave one on top of the pile of pinecones at the little girl's apartment. The next morning, it was gone.

My story ends anticlimactically... I moved away.

I never knew the girl's name, and she will never know mine.

We never met.

She will never know where those pinecones came from.

Like Boo Radley – I wanted to show her that I cared about her. I wanted her to know that I shared her love of pinecones.. and that something as simple as that is enough to join two lives together...

But most of all, I wanted her to experience a beautiful mystery in her life.

OLD GEEZER GRANDPA

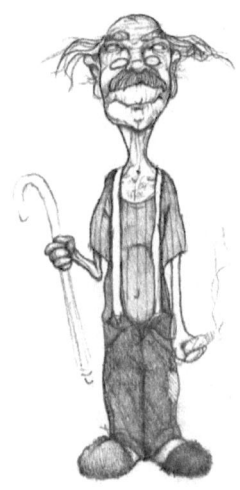

Once upon a time I lived in an apartment with my dog Gunther...

Mostly, I kept to myself – but I did manage to make one friend: An eleven-year-old boy named Tyler.

Tyler loved to watch me draw.

Often, we would sit together on the open patio outside my apartment (with Gunther at our feet) enjoying the afternoon.

Although I drew many things for Tyler – one day he made a special request.

"Can you draw an old geezer grandpa?" he asked.

"A what?" I replied. I wasn't sure I had heard him correctly.

"An old geezer grandpa!"

Not a dinosaur, or some exotic animal.. not a spaceship, or a super hero. Tyler was practically jumping up and down with excitement – he wanted an "old geezer grandpa"... so I drew him one.

Tyler hung over my shoulder – frantically giving directions.

"Give him a moustache! And glasses!" Tyler shouted.

We spent the afternoon that way..

Two infinitely different people

Separated by age and circumstance

Brought together

By the experience of art.

LETTER TO A YOUNG ARTIST

Dear little boy,

You may not have noticed, but I have been watching you grow.

I remember the first time you came into our art class. You were shy and quiet. You walked to the back of the room and sat at a table by yourself. When I gave you a pencil and a piece of paper, you told me you couldn't draw.

When you came back the following week, I was happy to see you. Again, when I gave you paper and a pencil, you told me you couldn't draw. I sat down and asked you to tell me about something you liked to do – something you were good at. You told me you liked to play soccer.

"Were you a terrific soccer player the first time you tried?

"No." you said.

"How did you get better?" I asked.

"I practiced."

"It's the same thing with drawing," I explained, "the more you draw, the better you'll get."

The following week you were back again. This time, you sat at a table next to my husband, Richard. I saw how intently you were watching him draw. You asked him to draw a truck. I watched as you tried to draw one by yourself.

The next time I saw you at class, you were sitting with the group, drawing everything in sight. The stuffed animals on the table, flowers and butterflies – even copying images from the mural on the wall. I could tell you had been practicing – a lot. I sat down next to you and told you how amazing your drawings were.

"Hey, I thought you said you couldn't draw!" I teased, gently.

You looked at me and smiled.

The following week we sat at a table and drew pictures together. I complimented your work – "Wow, that's a great hand. Hands are hard to do – I still have trouble with them, sometimes." You looked at my drawing and asked how I got to be so good. "Practice," I said, "Years and years of practice."

When class ended, you hugged me.

Dear little boy, you are an artist.

Soon our class will be over and you may never see me again..

but the gift you found within yourself will be with you always.

EMBRACING CHAOS AND THE ART OF OPEN DOORS

My husband and I teach art to a group of inner city kids... but that's not really what we do.

We do not have a traditional class where we see the same students every week.. sitting in designated places, teaching them a new lesson designed to progressively improve their drawing skills.

There are so many children.

Our class is growing constantly because we keep the door wide open.

I suppose I could simply shut the door and keep the size of the class to something more manageable..

But I would rather embrace the chaos than exclude a single child from the experience of making art.

So we squeeze together at the tables with our elbows bumping

passing out paper to anyone who joins us

sharing pencils, markers and crayons

drawing and talking together..

We may not be following a specific lesson plan

but these children are learning that when they want to express

themselves the door to art is always open.

VOLUNTEERING AND THE ART OF TIME TRAVEL

Recently, a friend told me of an exercise he read about several years ago. It had to do with empowering oneself within the memories of childhood. Basically, if you had a bad experience when you were a child, you could somehow change the outcome of it. It is an act of imagination – the "Now You" returns to help the "Little You".

An interesting idea.

Naturally, I found myself roaming through the memories of my own childhood

Now Me, looking for Little Me..

And then I stopped.

In a way, I am already doing this.

At the center where we volunteer..

I see myself in some of the kids in our art class.

The quiet ones.

The introverts.

The lonely and the ignored.

I seek them out

and I think that the words I would have spoken to Little Michele

are the same words that I share with them.

Time travel is possible, but it is not an act of imagination..

it is an act of love.

TEACHERS, ART AND THINGS THAT LAST FOREVER

When I was a child I would spend hours quietly playing by myself. Endlessly entertained by my wild imagination – I would stay up all night long drawing pictures. I was weird and solitary. My best friend was a dog.

School was difficult for intense, introverted kids like me.

It is so easy to become lost..

Sometimes, forever.

I don't remember much from those days.. after all, that was a very long time ago.

But I remember Mrs. Kelly – my elementary school art teacher.

Mrs. Kelly would sit next to me and quietly marvel over the drawings I made. Afterwards, she would put them in the glass display case in the hall outside her class – for all the world to see.

Now, volunteering to teach art to a group of inner city kids – I find myself drawn to the introverts. The quiet kids sitting alone.. trying to disappear into the background. I sit next to them. I draw with them. I speak quietly with them – and I marvel over the drawings they make.

If you are a teacher and think you do not make a difference – you are wrong.

You make all the difference in the world.

The time you give to your students can literally change the course of their lives. Your kindness and encouragement will echo inside them, and will continue to touch the lives of others forever.

Your reach is further than you can imagine.

Thank you, Mrs. Kelly... wherever you are.

I never got the chance to tell you that I love you.

MOTIVATION AND THE ART OF STARTING FIRES

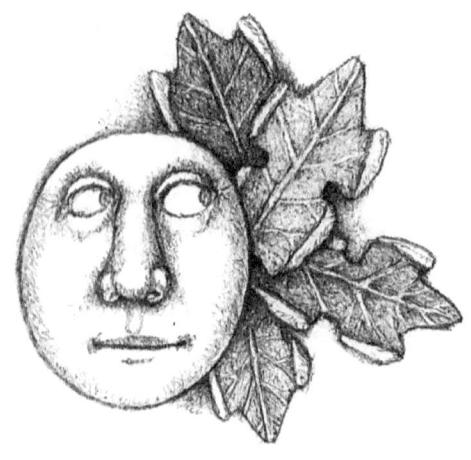

I dream of the butterfly effect..

To reach the heart of a single person

And set off the spark

That starts a fire.

HORRIBLE PAINTINGS AND THE ART OF HEALING

Practically all my paintings have been exhibited in galleries at one time or another. However, there is one that has never seen the light of day. I keep it shut in a closet, covered in an old t-shirt and facing the wall.

The reason I do this is because I need to keep it near me, but I don't want to see it... even accidentally. It is the painting I made around the time my father died. Heartbroken beyond all measure, I was able to let out into this painting what I could not express in emotion or words. It is a self-portrait — a painting so painful to look at it is almost unbearable.

Many years later, one of my sisters was going through a difficult period in her life — A sad, life-changing event that left her devastated. When she moved in with me and my husband, I had her room ready and waiting: A bed, a dresser, a place for her books and things.. and I hung that horrible painting on the wall.

She took one look at it and stopped dead in her tracks. Of course she asked me why I put that awful thing in her room.

I simply turned to her and said, "Look at me now."

As painful as it was, she immediately understood that she would get past this bad time in her life.

She had survived worse.

My sister kept that awful thing on her wall for a long time.

But, eventually..

as time heals all wounds,

she was ready to take the painting down.

Back into the closet it went.

NEXT DOOR NEIGHBORS AND THE ART OF FRIENDSHIP

When I was little, my sister's best friend lived in the house next door.

She spent a lot of time over there... and so did I.

Not to tag along like an annoying baby sister, though

I was there to see *my* friend, Vinny... Laura's father.

While Julie and Laura played upstairs

Vinny and I stayed in the kitchen.

What could we possibly have in common

to form such an unlikely bond with each other?

What did we have to say..

That would fill so many hours

Week after week?

Nothing, really.

We spent all our time drawing.

Our conversations took place in pictures passed back and forth across the table.

I invited him into my imagination — drawing weird creatures and anthropomorphic animals..

And he made me smile with pictures of rocking horses, racecars and trains.

Being so young, I did not understand the complexities of adulthood.

I didn't know that Vinny was dying.

I also didn't realize the depth of love and gratitude he felt for the little girl next door

who helped him rediscover his love of drawing

At a time when he needed it most.

PENCILS, PAPER AND THE ART OF GIVING GIFTS

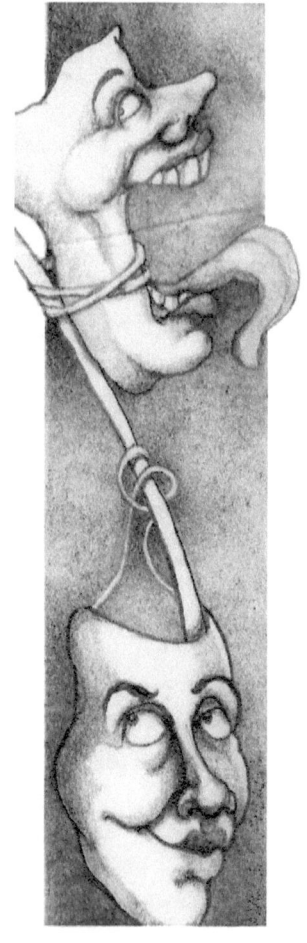

The day I discovered self-adhesive laminating sheets

Was the day I made hand-drawn bookmarks

for everyone I knew.

THE WOLF IN THE GALLERY

At the opening of one of my art exhibits I noticed a little girl wearing a wolf hat..

complete with pointed ears and furry paws dangling like a scarf on either side of her neck.

She was staring at me intensely from across the room.

The girl approached tentatively, waiting until I was alone..

"I really like your pictures." she said

I thanked her

And with a knowing smile

Asked the question I already knew the answer to..

"Do you like to draw?"

"Yes..." she said quietly

"But I am not as good as you."

Neither was I, I told her.

Not at first.

We spent the rest of the evening talking..

And after explaining how she never shows her drawings to anyone,

She asked if she could show them to me.

I gave her my email address

I would be honored.

A few days went by

And she sent me a pencil drawing

Pale gray and small.. It was a wolf, of course.

She assured me it would be okay if I didn't respond.

But I did..

Encouraging her

And admiring her imagination.

We exchanged several emails,

And she continued to send pictures..

horse-like dragons with triangle scales

Winged tigers with long eyelashes.

As time went on

The lines grew stronger, less tentative..

The animals took up more space on the page.

She did not have to tell me that my words gave her confidence

I saw it.

PAPER NAPKINS AND THE ART OF DINING OUT

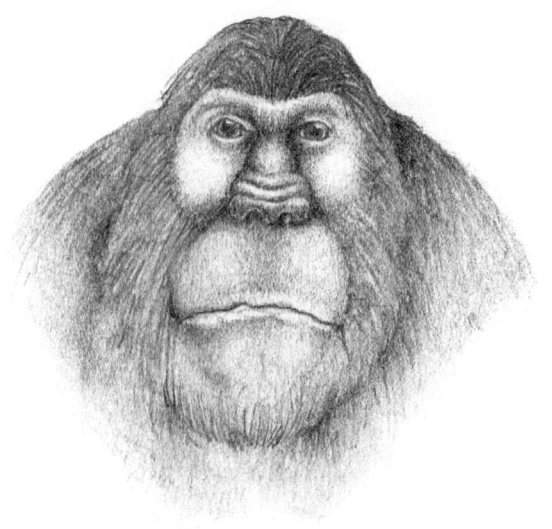

At restaurants

I like to draw on placemats and paper napkins..

Leaving behind little bits of beauty and weirdness wherever I go.

PAPER BUTTERFLIES AND THE ART OF CHANGING THE WORLD

I volunteer to teach art to a group of inner city kids in downtown Phoenix. In the summer, classes are longer and I am there for over three hours during the afternoon. Strange as it may sound, I like to go there unprepared. No lesson plan, no preconceived projects designed to hold their attention and occupy their time. Maybe that sounds crazy, but I have noticed that when I walk into that room with no expectations and an open heart, a lesson will unfold.

Sitting at tables drawing together, I spontaneously picked up a piece of paper and folded it into an origami butterfly. The girl sitting next to me asked if I would show her how to make one. "Yes," I told her.. "of course I will."

We moved onto the floor at the other end of the room, followed by two more girls. Step by step, the four of us slowly folded pieces of paper into butterflies. While we worked, I kept talking – stopping whenever someone got lost, backing up a few steps, gently encouraging them and taking the time to make sure everyone was following along.

"The first time is the hardest," I explained. "With each butterfly you make, it will get a little easier."

Sure enough, after about three or four butterflies, they were really getting the hang of it.

A group of other kids wandered over to where we were sitting and asked if I would teach them how to make butterflies, too. "Yes, of course," I replied - then I turned to my three butterfly-makers and said, "These are your teachers."

The girls looked at me, surprised. "You can do this," I told them. Then I grabbed a piece of paper and waited for the lesson to begin.

Throughout the day, more and more children came into the room – "Is this the origami class?" they would ask. Yes, I replied – welcoming them into the group. Every time a new student sat down, a new teacher would be there to help them learn. Each teacher that emerged, taught their students with the same gentleness, patience and encouragement that I first showed to the three little girls. I heard them softly repeat my words to each other, explaining how the first time is the hardest.. how with each butterfly, it will get a little easier.

Although I only taught three girls, about 40 kids learned how to make butterflies that day.

How can I even begin to explain how it felt to watch the chain-reaction that unfolded before me? Children as students, learning and becoming teachers; sharing their knowledge and empowering new teachers. Over and over, the cycle continued.. like the ripples of so many stones tossed into an endless river.

When I walked into that room I was a teacher. But when I became a student, a lesson unfolded with the delicate whisper of paper butterfly wings.. and the power to change the world.

SMALL MIRACLES AND THE ART OF TREMENDOUS CONSEQUENCES

My husband and I volunteer to teach art to a group of inner city kids in downtown Phoenix.

A couple of days ago, something miraculous occurred.

The room was filled with children – laughing, talking and drawing together.

I noticed a small boy sitting alone at a far table..

So still and quiet, he practically disappeared.

His head was bent down..

Intensely focused on the drawing in front of him.

I glanced at what he was working on

and I felt time stop.

All the chaos in the room faded into the background..

There was something different about this child.

Something rare and beautiful.

I saw it.

I *felt* it.

And in that seemingly small and insignificant moment..

I understood that there was something tremendous

in consequence

That brought me here.

"That is a great brontosaurus, "I told him

The boy looked up..

clearly surprised that I noticed him..

With a tiny smile, and light in his eyes

The boy whispered. "Thank you."

I asked him his name..

"Jesús." He replied.

I knelt down so we were face to face..

And looking directly into his eyes, I said

"Jesús, you have a gift from God."

ABOUT THE AUTHOR

MICHELE BLEDSOE is a self-taught artist and has been exhibiting her paintings and drawings in galleries for over 20 years. She is the co-author and illustrator of *The Secret Kingdom* – a children's book of paintings and poetry, and the illustrator of *Lemon Bee and Other Peculiar Tales* by author, Patricia Lynn Dompieri. Michele and her husband, artist Richard Bledsoe, live and paint happily together in Phoenix, Arizona.